DAYS OF DECISION

KT-471-248

Mandela and Truth and Reconciliation

30131 05297825 8

LONDON BOROUGH OF BARNET

Raintree is an imprint of Capstone Global Library Limited, a company incorporated in England and Wales having its registered office at 7 Pilgrim Street, London, EC4V 6LB – Registered company number: 6695582

www.raintreepublishers.co.uk
myorders@raintreepublishers.co.uk

Text © Capstone Global Library Limited 2014
First published in hardback in 2013
Paperback edition first published in 2014
The moral rights of the proprietor have been asserted.

All rights reserved. No part of this publication may be reproduced in any form or by any means (including photocopying or storing it in any medium by electronic means and whether or not transiently or incidentally to some other use of this publication) without the written permission of the copyright owner, except in accordance with the provisions of the Copyright, Designs and Patents Act 1988 or under the terms of a licence issued by the Copyright Licensing Agency, Saffron House, 6–10 Kirby Street, London EC1N 8TS (www.cla.co.uk). Applications for the copyright owner's written permission should be addressed to the publisher.

Edited by Andrew Farrow, Adrian Vigliano, and Mark Friedman
Designed by Cynthia Della-Rovere
Original illustrations © Capstone Global Library Ltd
Illustrated by H L Studios and Cynthia Della-Rovere
Picture research by Elizabeth Alexander
Production by Sophia Argyris
Originated by Capstone Global Library Ltd
Printed in China

ISBN 978 1 406 26152 3 (hardback)
17 16 15 14 13
10 9 8 7 6 5 4 3 2 1

ISBN 978 1 406 26159 2 (paperback)
17 16 15 14 13
10 9 8 7 6 5 4 3 2 1

British Library Cataloguing in Publication Data
A full catalogue record for this book is available from the British Library.

Acknowledgements
We would like to thank the following for permission to reproduce photographs: akg p. 14 (africanpictures); Corbis pp. 9 (Bettmann), 12 (Hulton-Deutsch Collection), 22 (Ulli Michel/Reuters), 29 (David Turnley), 36 (William Campbell/Sygma), 52, imprint (Reuters/ Scanfoto); Getty Images pp. 4, 33, 34 (Gallo Images/Oryx Media Archive), 21 (Roger Jackson/Central Press), 39, 42, 47 (Walter Dhladhla/AFP), 41 (Per-Anders Pettersson), 44 (Philip Littleton/AFP); Photoshot pp. 5 (Drum Social Histories), 24 (Greg Marinovich/South Photographs), 49 (Remi Ochlik/UPPA), 51t (Caroline Suzman/WpN/UPPA); Press Association Images pp. 11, 18 (AP Photo), 31 (AP Photo/ Nicky De Blois), 51b (Empics Sport); Rex Features pp. 16 (Sipa Press), 27 (Markus Zeffler).

Background and design features reproduced with the permission of Shutterstock (©Picsfive, ©Petrov Stanislav, ©Zastolskiy Victor, ©design36, ©a454).

Cover photograph of Nelson Mandela in 1990 reproduced with the permission of Corbis (© David Turnley); Cover photograph of a gathering outside a Truth and Reconciliation Commission hearing reproduced with the permission of Getty Images (Oryx Media Archive/Gallo Images).

We would like to thank Tabitha Kanogo for her invaluable help in the preparation of this book.

Every effort has been made to contact copyright holders of any material reproduced in this book. Any omissions will be rectified in subsequent printings if notice is given to the publisher.

Disclaimer
All the internet addresses (URLs) given in this book were valid at the time of going to press. However, due to the dynamic nature of the internet, some addresses may have changed, or sites may have changed or ceased to exist since publication. While the author and publisher regret any inconvenience this may cause readers, no responsibility for any such changes can be accepted by either the author or the publisher.

Contents

Some words are printed in **bold**, like this. You can find out what
they mean by looking in the glossary on page 60.

The first witness speaks out

It is 15 April 1996, the day of the very first public hearing of the Truth and **Reconciliation** Commission (TRC) in South Africa. The city hall in East London, Eastern Cape, is full to bursting with friends, family, and well-wishers who have come to hear witnesses' stories of the horrors they endured during the days of **apartheid**. Many thousands of other people in South Africa and around the world are tuning in on their televisions and radios.

Archbishop Desmond Tutu (centre), the chairman of the Truth and Reconciliation Commission, at the commission's first hearing in East London, South Africa.

A huge security force protects the gathering. This is ironic, because until very recently, police officers like these were the very people who carried out the beatings, torture, and killings the victims are about to describe. The atmosphere is tense. There has already been a bomb scare, forcing everyone to clear the hall, and no one quite knows how the day will proceed.

Archbishop Desmond Tutu, the leader of the Anglican Church in Cape Town and the chair of the commission, introduces the session with hymns and prayer, which calm the audience somewhat. He welcomes everyone in the room and around the world who has helped the commission, which is now "charged to unearth the truth about our dark past"[1]

Explaining what happened

Silence falls over the room as the first witness, Nohle Mohape, begins to speak. She states, "I am very happy today after 20 years to be present in this commission... I am very happy to get this chance to sit in front of you to explain to you who killed my husband."[2]

This is the first of more than 50 public hearings across South Africa, where many deeply emotional and horrific tales will be told.

President Nelson Mandela, the first black president of democratic South Africa, is the person responsible for beginning this extraordinary process. Imprisoned by previous South African governments for opposing white rule, Mandela firmly believes that South Africa should come to terms with its conflict-torn past. This book describes how important decisions about truth and reconciliation came to be made.

Nohle Mohape's story

In the 1970s, Nohle Mohape's husband, Mapetla, was active in the **Black Consciousness movement**, which urged black people to be proud of themselves and to resist the unjust apartheid policies. Mapetla had been in prison several times for his political activities. After he died in prison, the official verdict (judgement) was that he had committed suicide. But his wife knew that her husband had been determined to continue the struggle against apartheid. She was sure he was killed, explaining, "The letters which were available during the inquest [inquiry into the death], there was one amongst them of which it was said to be the suicide letter. The writing ... did not belong to Mapetla."

For her children's sake, Nohle Mohape concluded, "My hope is that the TRC ... will try to find out what happened ... so that when my children are elderly people, they will know exactly what happened to their father."[3]

Black South Africans had protested against white rule for decades. This photo from 1955 shows people demonstrating during Defiance Campaign against apartheid (see pages 8–9); many campaign leaders were arrested.

Mandela: an activist against apartheid

Nelson Mandela was born in 1918. His father was Chief Henry Mandela, a member of the Madiba clan. This clan was made up of the Xhosa-speaking Tembu people of Transkei, in South Africa. Nelson attended the South African Native College (later called Fort Hare University) where he studied law at the University of Witwatersrand from 1943 to 1948. He went on to pass an exam that allowed him to practise as a lawyer. It was quite remarkable for a young black man in South Africa to attend college or university at all at this time.

South Africa under white rule

After 1910, the Union of South Africa was formed, making it an independent country that was no longer ruled by the United Kingdom. Under its **constitution**, English-speaking white people and **Afrikaners** (people of European, mostly Dutch background) had complete political and economic control. Only white people could vote for white representatives in **parliament**.

The government also set aside most of the land for white people, who made up just 20 per cent of the population. Under the 1913 Natives' Land Act, only 7 per cent of South Africa's land could be settled by Africans (black people).[1] In 1936, land for Africans was increased to about 13 per cent.

Within the white population, the Afrikaners were at a disadvantage compared to the English-speaking whites. Most were poor farmers. In 1914, the **National Party (NP)** was established to campaign for the rights of Afrikaners. Due to the influence of the NP, between the 1920s and 1940s, the government created jobs for Afrikaners, and Afrikaners' political power grew. The Afrikaners aimed to rule South Africa.

The opposition

In 1912, black delegates (representatives) from the four provinces of the country formed the South African Native National Congress to campaign against the loss of their rights. From 1923, the organization was known as the African National Congress (ANC). The **South African Communist Party (SACP)** formed in 1921, also to fight for black rights. It had members of different races.

Meanwhile, black people, who had been deprived of their land, were forced to work for white businesses. For example, black miners toiled in diamond mines in horrendous conditions for low wages.

It was against this background that Nelson Mandela entered politics. In 1944, he decided to join an organization called the **African National Congress (ANC)**. Mandela became the leader of the ANC's Youth League. His commitment to black people's freedom would last his entire life.

Apartheid begins

Four years later, in 1948, the NP was elected to power. Its leader, Daniel François Malan, brought in the system of apartheid – a rigid separation of society based on race, centred around the idea that white people were superior to all other people. The Afrikaners were joined by English-speaking whites in dominating South Africa.

Racial groups

In South Africa, the four racial groups in apartheid were divided as follows:

- *White*: The white group included people of European origin, including English-speaking whites and Afrikaners.

- *Coloured*: The **coloured** group included people of mixed race, with a black and a white parent.

- *Asiatic*: The Asiatic group included people of Indian origin (around 2 to 3 per cent of the population).

- *Native*: The native group included Africans (black people) – the native people of South Africa.

Key:
---------- Boundary of the Union of South Africa, from 1910

0 miles 200
0 km 200

Rhodesia
Portuguese East Africa
Bechuanaland
Transvaal
Great Namaland
Soweto
Kliptown
Sharpeville
Boipatong
Pretoria
Johannesburg
Vereeniging
Swaziland
Orange Free State
Natal
Orange River
Basutoland
South Africa
Durban
Robben Island
Cape of Good Hope
Transkei
Kwazulu
Ciskei
Bisho
King William's Town
East London
Indian Ocean
Atlantic Ocean
Worcester
Cape Town
N

This map of South Africa under apartheid shows the main places mentioned in this book. The neighbouring countries were also under white rule, but South Africa was the last to move to democracy.

Under apartheid, the population was categorized into four races, who were to live, work, and socialize separately. Whites were to be at the top, running the country, while black people would be at the bottom of the pile. Whites benefited from excellent housing, education systems, and public transport. But the black majority were to live in **Bantustans**, the areas they originally came from. For example, if you were Xhosa, you were to live in the Transkei Bantustan. In the Bantustans, land was poor and there were few facilities.

The Defiance Campaign

Apartheid turned black people into prisoners in their own country, with all their freedoms removed. They had to carry a "pass book" (identity paper) at all times. Black people had to observe a curfew, staying indoors from late evening until morning. They were forbidden to enter whites-only areas and public facilities. Yet resistance to apartheid soon developed, and Mandela played a key role.

Mandela and non-violence

Mandela had great respect for the Indian independence leader Mahatma Gandhi, but Mandela did not share Gandhi's belief in non-violence as the only possible method of resistance. Reflecting back on the Defiance Campaign, Mandela commented: "I saw non-violence on the Gandhian model not as an inviolable principle [principle that must always be followed] but as a tactic to be used as the situation demanded."[3] He felt that it was better to secure change without violence if possible, but if a non-violent campaign failed, new tactics would be needed.

In 1952, the ANC and the South African Indian Congress (an organization that fought for the rights of the Indian community in South Africa) called for a Defiance Campaign against the apartheid laws. It was a campaign of non-violent protest to demonstrate the unfairness of the rules. The idea came from the non-violent struggle led by Mahatma Gandhi against Britain's rule in India. This was popular with South African Indians and

SLEGS BLANKES
EUROPEANS ONLY

During the 1952 Defiance Campaign, black people in Cape Town took over a train carriage marked "Europeans only". The police arrested them on arrival.

influenced Mandela at the time. Mandela travelled around South Africa, building support for the campaign.

During the Defiance Campaign, black protesters publicly burnt their pass books, deliberately went into white areas, stayed out after curfew time, and climbed aboard whites-only train carriages. The police arrested thousands of demonstrators. For example, Mandela and 52 others were arrested for walking through a white area of Johannesburg at 11 p.m.[2]

Legal aid for the powerless

In addition to protesting, Mandela also wanted to provide practical help for black people who were struggling in their daily lives. In a courageous move, he and another black lawyer, Oliver Tambo, established South Africa's first black law practice in Johannesburg in 1952. The pair offered low-cost legal aid and assisted black people who had broken the apartheid laws. Mandela could probably have made more money doing something else, but he was committed to helping his people.

Banning orders

Following the Defiance Campaign, Mandela, like other leading campaigners, had received **banning orders** that forbade him from leaving Johannesburg, making speeches, or attending meetings. Despite being banned from speaking and moving freely, Mandela developed a way for ANC members to communicate secretly and quickly through a network of people, even without holding public meetings. Mandela showed great foresight. A modified version of his secret communication plan would later be adopted after the ANC was banned.

The Freedom Charter

Despite the banning orders preventing them from speaking out, anti-apartheid leaders remained determined to openly challenge the law. In 1955, Mandela participated in the Congress of the People in Kliptown, near Johannesburg. It was organized by several groups, among them the ANC, the South African Indian Congress, the South African Coloured People's Organization, and the South African Congress of **Trade Unions**. The gathering attracted over 3,000 people.

Mandela helped to draft the Freedom **Charter** that was taken up by the congress. The Freedom Charter was a call for equal rights for all in a multiracial **democracy**. Mandela was already used to campaigning alongside people from different racial backgrounds and was committed to working with all South Africans – including white people.

What do you think?

Was the Freedom Charter a threat to the government?

The Freedom Charter states that there should be democracy in South Africa, giving equal rights to all people. It says:

"We, the people of South Africa, declare for all our country and the world to know:

That South Africa belongs to all who live in it, black and white, and that no government can justly claim authority unless it is based on the will of all the people…

That only a democratic state, based on the will of all the people, can secure to all their birthright [basic right] without distinction of colour, race, sex or belief."[4]

Why do you think many white South Africans objected to the charter?

The treason trial

The government reacted strongly to the Freedom Charter, seeing it as a threat to the nation. The police were sent to the Congress of the People to search for evidence that representatives there were plotting against the government. Using the information gathered, in December 1956, the government arrested 156 leaders of the anti-apartheid movement, of all races. It charged them with **treason** and with being **communists**. If sentenced, the leaders could be executed (killed). The trial dragged on until 1961, when all the accused were acquitted (proven not guilty) of the charges. At the trial, Mandela's clear, careful statements demonstrated that he had become an able political leader.

Nelson Mandela (on the right) singing with supporters and other accused people during the treason trial in Johannesburg, in 1956.

Lilian Ngoyi 1911–1980

Born: Pretoria, Transvaal, South Africa
Role: Politician and anti-apartheid activist

Lilian Ngoyi worked in a clothing factory as a machinist from 1945 to 1956. She joined the ANC during the Defiance Campaign and was arrested for going to the white people's area of a post office. Ngoyi became president of the ANC Women's League in 1953 and president of the Federation of South African Women in 1956. She travelled abroad to win support for the anti-apartheid movement, addressing protest meetings around the world. Ngoyi led a women's anti-pass march in Pretoria in December 1956, to protest against a law requiring women to carry passes. She was one of 156 leading activists arrested for treason and spent five months in prison in 1960. Ngoyi lived under banning orders for much of the 1960s and 1970s, which kept her in her house and prevented her from attending gatherings.[5]

Did you know? Ngoyi died two months before her last banning order was due to end.[6]

Violent struggle

In 1958, Hendrik Verwoerd became South Africa's new **prime minister**. Verwoerd was devoted to apartheid, and he was angered by the failure of the Bantustan policy (see page 8). Instead of moving to the Bantustans, many black people had settled in **townships** on the edge of white cities so that they could access jobs easily. Verwoerd became determined to push Africans out of the cities and away from the white population.

The anti-apartheid movement splits

During the late 1950s, the anti-apartheid movement was equally determined to fight the government's Bantustan policy, but there were arguments about how best to do this.

Some ANC leaders, including Mandela and Walter Sisulu, were committed to working with organizations of different racial groups, including coloured and Indian groups, as well as white organizations such as the SACP and the Congress of Democracy (which supported equal rights for all).

Yet some black activists felt strongly that the anti-apartheid movement should contain only black people, who should rely on their own resources to struggle for freedom. Under the leadership of Robert Sobukwe, these campaigners formed the **Pan Africanist Congress (PAC)** in 1959, splitting the anti-apartheid movement.

The scene after the Sharpeville massacre, with dead and injured people strewn on the ground. The protesters had not been armed but were shot by the police.

Sharpeville massacre

In 1960, both the ANC and PAC organized protests against the pass laws that restricted black people's freedom of movement. One such protest took place in March in Sharpeville, a black township near Vereeniging. People left their pass books at home and demonstrated outside the police station. Fights broke out between the police and protesters, and some police officers were injured.

In panic, the police, according to one report, "opened fire with sub-machine guns, Sten guns [light machine guns], and rifles, and eyewitnesses said that the front ranks of the crowd fell like ninepins [bowling pins]... Mangled bodies of men, women and children lay sprawled on the roadway." After the **massacre**, 69 protesters lay dead.[1] Disgusted by this demonstration of police brutality, black people around the country took to the streets in strikes and demonstrations. In this atmosphere of heightened tension, the government banned the ANC and PAC.

Decisive words: Mandela and the armed struggle

In June 1961, the meeting of the ANC Working Committee (made up of leading ANC members) discussed whether to adopt a policy of armed struggle. Mandela used an African saying to compare the strength of the apartheid state – "the wild beast" – to unarmed black people, who needed to defend themselves more forcefully, saying:

"I was candid [open] and explained why I believed we had no choice but to turn to violence. I used an old African expression: '*Sebatana ha se bokwe ka diatla*' ('The attacks of the wild beast cannot be averted [prevented] with only bare hands')."[3]

Sabotage

The Sharpeville massacre affected Mandela deeply. He came to believe that non-violent methods were not bringing results. Mandela now decided to abandon non-violent protest and called for acts of **sabotage** against the **regime**. He felt it was time to fight violence with violence. He also realized that activists were becoming fed up with the ANC leadership's non-violent stance and were likely to switch to violent tactics anyway. Mandela thought it was better to take control to avoid loss of life, declaring: "Would it not be better to guide this violence ourselves, according to principles where we save lives by attacking symbols of oppression [cruel, unfair treatment], and not people?"[2]

Sabotage!

In 1961, Mandela helped to found the military wing of the ANC, Umkhonto we Sizwe (MK). This armed group carried out sabotage attacks, damaging the property of the South African government. It did not intend to harm people.

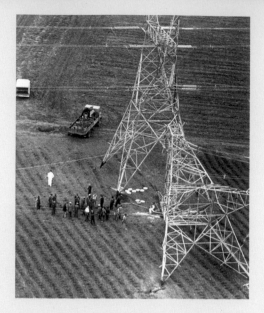

As the leader of an illegal armed force, Mandela was now at risk of arrest, imprisonment, and even the death sentence. He had to go "underground" to avoid arrest, meaning he was hiding in the homes of friends and sympathizers and constantly moving from place to place. Realizing he needed to learn to use violent tactics, in 1962 he travelled to Algeria, in northwest Africa, where he trained in sabotage and guerrilla warfare, which is when an irregular group of fighters wages war against a normal army.

This photo shows damaged electrical equipment at a power station following a sabotage bombing attack by MK members.

Mandela's friends warned him not to return to South Africa, because the police would track him down there. He could have

Sabotage in South Africa

The following is a brief history of sabotage in South Africa:

- Starting in 1961, MK launched a sabotage campaign. Activists bombed power stations, government buildings, and transport facilities.

- The PAC established its own military wing, Poqo (meaning "Pure" or "Alone" in Xhosa), to carry out similar attacks. It referred to the belief that Africans should fight for **liberation** alone, without collabourating with other groups.

- In 1962, the South African government brought in a new, harsh law to try to stop the attacks. People who committed acts of sabotage could be punished with the death penalty.

- By late 1964, the government had managed to stop the sabotage movement.

chosen a life in **exile**. But Mandela decided he had to be with his people to participate in the struggle from within the country.

Mandela: arrest and prison

After his return to South Africa, Mandela was not as secretive about his movements as he could have been. He would pop up in public places, and people would recognize him. In August 1962, the police succeeded in finding and arresting him. Was this partly his own fault for not being more careful?

The police arrested several other ANC leaders, too. In the Rivonia trial of 1964, the leaders were all tried for sabotage, treason, and violent conspiracy (secret plans to do illegal deeds). For the second time, Mandela escaped the death sentence. But on 12 June 1964, he was sentenced to life imprisonment.

Decisive words: Mandela's trial speech

On 20 April 1964, at the start of the court case against him, Mandela made a long, powerful speech justifying his actions. Here, he carefully explains why MK was set up:

"All lawful modes of expressing opposition to this principle [of white supremacy] had been closed by legislation [law-making], and we were placed in a position in which we had either to accept a permanent state of inferiority, or to defy the government. We chose to defy the law. We first broke the law in a way which avoided any recourse to violence; when this form was legislated against, and then the government resorted to a show of force to crush opposition to its policies, only then did we decide to answer violence with violence.

But the violence which we chose to adopt was not terrorism."[4]

What do you think?

Could armed struggle be justified?

Was it sensible for the ANC to take up armed struggle so that it could control the violence and avoid death or injury? Or was using violence morally wrong because it made the ANC just as bad as the apartheid government?

The tide turns

In 1964, Mandela – along with other political prisoners – was imprisoned on Robben Island, an island west of the coast of Cape Town. He could not have anticipated just how long he would spend in prison. Mandela greatly missed his wife, Winnie, and would always regret not being able to watch his family grow up, feeling he had failed in his responsibilities towards them.

The conditions on Robben Island were miserable. Prisoners were forced to do backbreaking work crushing stones, and they complained about the dreadful food. However, the prisoners made the

The courtyard of Robben Island prison in the mid-1960s. The line of prisoners on the right are mending old clothes, an activity organized by prison officials to impress visitors.

Mandela: a man of principle

At times, Mandela was offered freedom under certain conditions, but he always took a principled stand and refused the option:

- In 1976, the government said it would free him if he recognized the independence of the Transkei Bantustan and agreed, as a Xhosa (a member of a group of people from southeast South Africa), to live there. But most black people opposed the Bantustan policy. Mandela refused to move to the Transkei, which would have implied that he accepted the policy.[2]

- In 1985, Mandela refused the offer of freedom in return for giving up the armed struggle. He insisted that the government would have to cease using violence against the anti-apartheid movement first.

best of their terrible situation. They used the opportunity to read and study. Some who entered prison unable to read eventually left with degrees.

A leader in prison

Mandela spent his time in prison getting to know all the other prisoners and guards. He studied law and read widely, including the works of great world leaders of all political viewpoints, in order to understand how they operated. He also focused on the politics and literature of the Afrikaners, in order to try to understand their thinking.

Since prisoners and guards lived closely together, Mandela came to know his Afrikaner guards extremely well. In some ways, he saw the guards as being imprisoned, too – in their jobs and way of thinking – and he made a conscious decision to understand their position rather than confront them. The guards tended to be young, uneducated Afrikaners from poor backgrounds. They had never made friends with black people before. Soon they deferred to Mandela, with his natural leadership qualities, and came to him to discuss their own problems. Mandela even made the effort to learn the **Afrikaans** language, although fellow prisoner Ahmed Kathrada later joked that Mandela had a terrible accent![1]

Understanding the Afrikaners

As part of his leadership role in prison, Mandela encouraged other political prisoners on Robben Island to learn Afrikaans and talk to the Afrikaners. At first, SACP activist Mac Maharaj was anti-Afrikaans and wanted nothing to do with Afrikaners, but he came to see the wisdom of Mandela's advice, saying:

> "I realized the importance of learning Afrikaans history, of reading Afrikaans literature, of trying to understand these ordinary men… how they are indoctrinated [forced to accept a set of beliefs], how they react. They all have a blank wall in their minds. They just could not see the black man as a human being."[3]

Among the political prisoners, Mandela held a leadership position, and he also received the advice and support of other imprisoned ANC leaders. He acted as their spokesperson, lodging complaints with the commissioner (head) of prisons about conditions and leading campaigns for improvements. Mandela also continued to work with the ANC outside, through secret contacts with Oliver Tambo, who was heading the ANC in exile.

Apartheid under pressure

In the 1960s and 1970s, opposition to South Africa's apartheid system mounted. In this era, many African countries secured their independence from colonial rule (being ruled by other countries), and they supported the anti-apartheid movement. Campaigns arose in Western countries, including the movement to stop economic and sports links with South Africa.

Black Consciousness and the Soweto Uprising

Within South Africa, in the 1970s, the Black Consciousness movement became influential. A man called Steve Biko started the movement among black students. The movement urged black people to be proud of their race and not imitate white people.

In June 1976, young people in the Black Consciousness movement protested. Angry about being

Decisive words: Steve Biko and black pride

Steve Biko's writings were collected in a book published after his death called *I Write What I Like*. In the following passage, he speaks of the responsibility of black people to shake off their negative image of themselves, saying:

"It becomes more necessary to see the truth as it is if you realise that the only vehicle for change are these people who have lost their personality. The first step therefore is to make the black man come to himself; to pump back life into his empty shell; to infuse [fill] him with pride and dignity."[5]

Hundreds of people took to the streets during the Soweto protests against the use of Afrikaans in school teaching. The people of Soweto took a leading role in the campaign for black equality.

forced to learn half of their classes in Afrikaans, thousands of pupils in the township of Soweto, near Johannesburg, took to the streets. The police opened fire, killing two demonstrators. One of them was 12-year-old Hector Pieterson. After shots rang out, his sister Antoinette saw him being scooped up by a stranger – and then she saw the blood. Hector died later that day.[4]

After the shocking killings, further protests around the country ensued. Then, in August 1977, the police arrested Biko. At the police station, they beat him so badly that he fell into a coma and died within five days.

On Robben Island, Mandela heard about the uprising from newly arrived prisoners. These younger black men, many linked to the Black Consciousness movement, sparked discussions with Mandela about the way forwards for the anti-apartheid struggle. He listened carefully to the views of these young activists, even though he did not always agree with them. They came to respect the way he encouraged all the political prisoners to cooperate, despite their different political views.

White protests

Meanwhile, some white South Africans were also actively campaigning against apartheid, including a number of church leaders, women's and student groups, and novelists. Starting in 1978, the new prime minister, P.W. Botha, brought in some reforms to try to calm the situation. For example, in 1979, he permitted black people to form trade unions. Yet the reforms merely increased the desire of anti-apartheid campaigners for deeper changes.

Fighting apartheid from prison

News was slow to reach the prisoners on Robben Island, and it was hard for Mandela to communicate with the outside world because his letters were censored, which means that parts considered a political threat were removed. When news of the Soweto Uprising finally reached Mandela through a new prisoner in August 1976, Mandela wrote a statement expressing fervent support for the revolt and inspiring confidence in the protesters. He wrote: "Unite! Mobilise! Fight On! Between the anvil of united mass action and the hammer of armed struggle we shall crush apartheid."[6]

Mac Maharaj smuggled out the document when he was released from Robben Island in December that year. The regular smuggling of documents allowed Mandela to engage with the anti-apartheid struggle from behind bars and to continue his leadership role.

The 1980s: the people rise up

In 1983, Prime Minister Botha attempted to divide the opposition to apartheid. He introduced a new constitution that offered some political rights to coloured people and Indians, but it still left out the black population. The new constitution also ensured that white people kept political control (see the box on the right).

In an angry response to the new constitution, more than 500 anti-apartheid groups, including churches, trade unions, community associations, and student organizations, formed a broad alliance called the **United Democratic Front (UDF)**. The UDF organized **boycotts** (for example, refusing to pay rent), demonstrations, and acts of sabotage. In 1985, the Congress of South African Trade Unions (COSATU) formed to coordinate the activities of the new black trade unions, which had thousands of members.

The new constitution of 1983

Many Afrikaner leaders realized that they would have to alter the apartheid system. Botha hoped that changing the constitution would solve the crisis. He maintained that black people had their own **homelands** where they had rights, so they did not require rights in all of South Africa. Since the Indian and coloured people lacked homelands, the new constitution provided a house of parliament for each of them. There were now three houses of parliament, but the members of the white parliament outnumbered the other two, so they retained most of the power. The entire non-white community rejected the new constitution.

The government responded to this show of opposition. The move merely strengthened the protest. Botha then attempted to crush the movement with force. In 1985, he declared a State of Emergency, allowing the government to restrict freedoms as a way to keep order. The government banned organizations and placed activists under house arrest (confined them to their homes). The police and army arrested and tortured thousands more. Yet nothing could stop the tide of opposition to apartheid.

The international anti-apartheid movement stepped up its activities, too. By 1986, many nations had imposed **economic sanctions** on South Africa, refusing to trade or invest money there. This movement demanded that Botha's government free Mandela and end apartheid.

P.W. Botha 1916–2006

Born: Paul Roux, Orange Free State, South Africa

Role: Prime minister (1978–1984) and state president (1984–1989) of South Africa

P.W. Botha became a full-time organizer for the NP when he was just 20 years old, and he was elected to parliament in 1948. He worked in various government departments and became prime minister in 1978. Botha sent South African forces to raid newly independent southern African countries, to weaken their governments and stop them from supporting the anti-apartheid movement. Within South Africa, he tried to separate the black homelands from South Africa by granting them independence, in order to maintain white rule in the rest of South Africa. But the non-white population continued to resist the government, and Botha responded by treating opposition groups brutally. Botha was summoned before the TRC in 1997, but he refused to take part.

Did you know? South Africans nicknamed Botha the "Great Crocodile" because of his aggressive nature.

The ANC clashes with Inkatha

The anti-apartheid movement was not completely united, though. Within South Africa, the ANC clashed with the **Inkatha** movement in the KwaZulu Bantustan, led by the Zulu leader Mangosutho Buthelezi. Buthelezi opposed apartheid, but he refused to work with the ANC. The disagreement led to violent confrontations. It was later discovered that the government had backed Inkatha, in order to increase this violence and divide the opposition to apartheid.[7]

In London, on 21 March 1970, members of the anti-apartheid movement marked the tenth anniversary of the Sharpeville massacre.

Negotiating democracy

Even at the height of most conflicts, representatives of the warring parties will often hold talks to see if they can overcome the gulf between them. In 1988, Mandela, now in Pollsmoor Prison, came up with a plan to enter private negotiations with members of Botha's government. Although in prison, Mandela was a respected leader of the ANC, possessing the authority to begin discussions on behalf of the anti-apartheid movement.

Mandela strongly believed that it was possible to reach a peaceful settlement. Eventually, he met Botha himself, and in 1989, he met with the new president, F.W. de Klerk. Some radical ANC leaders disagreed with Mandela's approach. They thought it was necessary to continue the armed struggle and seize the government by force. They feared that negotiations would leave power in white hands.

Why was Mandela confident this path would succeed? He had befriended many Afrikaners and knew he could work with them. For its part, the government now realized that Mandela, although languishing in prison for sabotage and treason, held the key to a successful shift to democracy. Senior

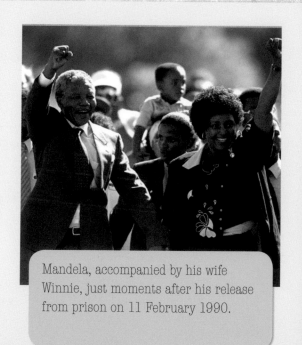

Mandela, accompanied by his wife Winnie, just moments after his release from prison on 11 February 1990.

Dismantling apartheid

The following timeline shows the events that led to the end of apartheid from 1990 to 1994:

1989	1990	1991
13 December	**2 February**	De Klerk repeals the remaining apartheid laws
De Klerk meets with Mandela	De Klerk lifts the ban on anti-apartheid organizations and releases political prisoners	

government figures realized that they had to include the majority population – black people – in the government to prevent chaos. The government needed Mandela for its own survival.

Freedom

In 1990, de Klerk made several historic decisions. He overturned the ban on the ANC, PAC, and SACP, and on 11 February, he released Mandela from prison. After more than 10,000 days in captivity, Mandela walked free, accompanied by his wife, Winnie. Raising their fists in the ANC salute, they were greeted by ecstatic onlookers, both black and white, while millions around the world watched on television. Mandela was whisked off to City Hall in Cape Town to make his first public speech since 1964. The world wondered: would this 71-year-old former prisoner now lead his country?

Mandela took over from Oliver Tambo as president of the ANC in July 1991. He faced the tricky task of leading the ANC negotiations with de Klerk to end apartheid and introduce a democratic government. In December 1991, the government set up the Convention for a Democratic South Africa (CODESA) to begin the talks.

F.W. de Klerk

Born: Johannesburg, South Africa, 1936

Role: President of South Africa, 1989–1994

In 1989, F.W. de Klerk was elected leader of the NP and president of South Africa. He became committed to ending apartheid and met with Mandela. After releasing Mandela and other political prisoners and lifting bans on anti-apartheid organizations, de Klerk's government overturned the apartheid laws. In 1993, the NP reached an agreement with the ANC on the transfer to majority rule. De Klerk ensured that the white population would still have representation. After the 1994 election, he became second deputy president; he resigned in 1996.

1991
20 December
CODESA talks begin

1992
26 September
The government and the ANC sign a Record of Understanding

1994
27 April
The ANC wins the first multiracial elections

1994
10 May
Mandela becomes the president of South Africa

Democracy or civil war?

De Klerk sought the permission of the white population to continue negotiating with the ANC to dismantle apartheid. In a referendum (vote on a single issue) in March 1992, 69 per cent of voters supported these negotiations.[1]

However, tensions between the ANC and a group called the **Inkatha Freedom Party (IFP)** threatened to derail the process. The IFP was formed in July 1990, when Buthelezi turned his Inkatha movement (see page 21) into a political party. The IFP opposed a democratic government for a united South Africa, insisting instead on an independent KwaZulu homeland.

Mandela did his best to reach an understanding with Buthelezi. A week after he was freed, he visited Buthelezi and addressed a rally in the Zulu stronghold of Durban. He appealed to the crowd, saying: "Take your guns, your knives and your pangas [heavy knives] and throw them into the sea!" But Inkatha continued to oppose the ANC.[2]

In June 1992, aiming to cause instability and to disrupt progress toward democracy, Inkatha activists raided the township of Boipatong, near Vereeniging, killing 45 people. The police did nothing. The ANC suspected government involvement through a "third force"– meaning government-sponsored security forces were backing the IFP in order to fuel violence between black people.[3] So, the ANC suspended negotiations. How could Mandela negotiate with a government that was killing his people?

Then, in September, there was another massacre of ANC supporters, this

In one of the many clashes between IFP supporters and their opponents in the early 1990s, Inkatha members beat a non-Inkatha Freedom Party man they claimed shot at them previously.

The Forces in South Africa

In the early 1990s, the following forces were in favour of a multiracial government in South Africa:

- National Party (NP): The government in power, members of the NP, hoped to negotiate an end to apartheid but also to ensure that white interests would still be represented and protected.

- African National Congress (ANC): The ANC aimed to come to an agreement with the NP to establish democratic rule.

The following forces were against a multiracial government:

- The Volksfront: Formed in 1993, the Volksfront was an alliance of right-wing (conservative) groups, including the Afrikaner Weerstandsbeweging (AWB), that demanded a separate Afrikaner nation.

- The Inkatha Freedom Party (IFP): The IFP wanted KwaZulu to be an independent Zulu homeland.

- The "third force": An unofficial force was made up of government security forces; it backed the IFP and encouraged violence between the IFP and the ANC, in an attempt to prevent negotiations.

time in Bisho in the Ciskei, a black homeland in the Eastern Cape. In response, the ANC and the government signed a Record of Understanding to try to prevent more deaths. The Inkatha attacks declined. The ANC believed that the government's security forces were now able to rein in the IFP.

Mandela also worked hard to reach an agreement with the Afrikaners, assuring them that they would share power in the new South Africa. Some in the ANC criticized Mandela for offering them too much power. But what choice did he have? At the time, the Afrikaners controlled the police and security forces and could have resisted a complete takeover by the ANC. Additionally, they had the experience of running those services. It seemed preferable to come to a friendly agreement with the Afrikaners.

In April 1994, the ANC won the first multiracial election, and Mandela became the first black president. His **cabinet** included six NP and three IFP ministers. (Buthelezi became minister of home affairs.[4]) South Africa had its first democratically elected government.

Setting up the Truth and Reconciliation Commission

With a history of racial conflict, how could the people of South Africa come to terms with the past and move on? Bitter enemies now had to live and work together as equals. Mandela's cabinet included leading members of the ANC alongside the white politicians who had imprisoned them. Minister of Defence Joe Modise, the former commander of MK, would now cooperate with head of defence forces, General Georg Meiring, an Afrikaner who had brutally attacked black activists in the past. White police officers who had arrested, beaten, and tortured black people would now work alongside black officers in a multiracial police force.

The shoe is on the other foot

Many Afrikaners found it hard to accept that they were no longer in charge of the country. One Afrikaner farmer found that the theft of sheep from his farm had increased five times since the 1994 election. He now patrolled his property with a gun. He explained: "I am learning to fight, to kill, to hate. And we have nowhere to turn. Some years ago we could pick up the phone and talk to the highest power in the country. Now my home town is run by a guy whose name I can't even pronounce." This farmer expressed the same sense of powerlessness that millions of black Africans had felt for generations.[3]

Amnesty or war crimes trials?

The people negotiating on behalf of the former government wanted to simply put the past behind them. They requested a general **amnesty** – a pardon for everyone involved in running the apartheid system. However, members of the liberation movement believed that ignoring the past would imply forgetting the victims. By failing to acknowledge their pain and suffering, these people would be victimized once more.

At first, most people in the anti-apartheid movement thought the apartheid government should be made accountable, by bringing its leaders to **war crimes** trials. People looked back to the example set after World War II (1939–1945). After this war, leading **Nazis** were tried for war crimes in Nuremberg, Germany. Of the 19 who were convicted, 12 were sentenced to death, and the remainder were imprisoned.[1]

However, Germany had just been defeated in war, and the victorious nations chose to put key Nazis on trial. In South Africa, the supporters and opponents of apartheid had to learn to coexist. It would have been extremely difficult to put a Nuremberg option into practice. The police and military forces, which had implemented apartheid, would have opposed it. War crimes trials could have caused further resentment or even led to **civil war**.

This queue of people are waiting to vote in South Africa's first multiracial election. After the ANC won the election, Mandela included six NP and three IFP ministers in his government.

Discussing the options

To avoid potential problems, some people who had at first supported war crimes trials came to see the need for a different process. Mandela opted to consult widely rather than imposing a decision himself. The new government asked the public and the international community for ideas.

After hearing the results of the public dialogue over the issue, in 1993, the National Executive Committee (NEC) of the ANC announced the setting up of a special commission, stating: "The most important reason for the establishment of such a commission is to get to the truth."[2] The Truth and Reconciliation Commission (TRC) would acknowledge victims' experiences. It would also give amnesty to some **perpetrators** – meaning it would allow them to go free – if they made a full confession of their crimes. Without the amnesty condition, it would be hard to persuade the perpetrators to tell the whole truth.

Amnesty: a controversial option

Offering amnesty to perpetrators encouraged them to tell the truth. But at the same time, it allowed people who had committed terrible crimes to go unpunished. For example, Joe Slovo's wife, Ruth First, an anti-apartheid activist, had been killed by a letter bomb. When Slovo heard about the amnesty agreement, he said, "Now I know that my wife's killers will go free." It appeared to be an injustice to victims to see the murderers of their loved ones go free in return for confessing their crimes. Slovo's daughter Gillian was shocked, too, but she acknowledged, "The TRC was never supposed to be about justice; it's about the truth."[4]

Ubuntu: restoring harmony

The TRC was meant to promote healing relationships rather than retribution (punishment). There was a strong African foundation for this process: the idea of Ubuntu, or mutual humanity.

Archbishop Desmond Tutu explained this in 1996, saying:

> "God has given us a great gift, Ubuntu… Ubuntu says I am human only because you are human. If I undermine your humanity, I dehumanize myself. You must do what you can to maintain this great harmony, which is perpetually [continually] undermined by resentment, anger, desire for vengeance. That's why African jurisprudence [legal theory] is restorative [healing] rather than retributive [vengeful]."[5]

At hearings, the perpetrators would confess their crimes to the victims or their families, to make a clean break with the past. Victims' families would learn what had happened to their loved ones. It would not bring them back, but at least they would know the truth, allowing them to move on with their lives. Some families might feel able to forgive the perpetrators.

Timeline of the TRC
The following timeline highlights the major developments of the TRC:

1992	1993	1995
Mandela sets up a consultation group to discuss a truth commission	The ANC decides to set up a truth commission	The Promotion of National Unity and Reconciliation Act 34 establishes the Truth and Reconciliation Commission (TRC)

Desmond Tutu

Born: Klerksdorp, South Africa, 1931

Role: Archbishop of Cape Town; chair of the TRC

Desmond Tutu became an Anglican priest in 1961. In 1978, he was appointed the general secretary of the South African Council of Churches. Tutu worked tirelessly to draw worldwide attention to the injustices of apartheid. He focused on non-violent protest and promoted international economic sanctions to put pressure on the South African government. He became the first black archbishop of Cape Town in 1986. In 1995, he was appointed the head of the TRC, and he played a vital role in guiding the commission in its complex and difficult work.

Did you know? Tutu has a remarkable talent for bringing people together. In 1993, at the funeral of murdered SACP leader Chris Hani, Tutu succeeded in leading the angry crowd of 120,000 people to chant: "We will be free, all of us, black and white together!"[6]

Ubuntu fit with Mandela's personal commitment to forgiveness and reconciliation. It suited the situation, too, because the people of South Africa had to live together. Once Mandela had resolved to back the TRC, his support remained firm.

Archbishop Desmond Tutu at a rally in 1994. In 1984, he had received the Nobel Prize for Peace for his role in opposing apartheid in non-violent ways, so he was an ideal person to lead the reconciliation process.

1996	1997	1998	2003
The commission's public hearings begin	Winnie Mandela appears before the TRC. P.W. Botha refuses to appear.	The commission hearings end. The TRC's report is published.	Victims finally receive **compensation**

Setting up the commission

On 27 May 1994, Minister of Justice Dullah Omar announced to parliament the decision to set up the Truth and Reconciliation Commission (TRC). He made it clear that priority would be given to victims in the process, saying: "Disclosure of the truth and its acknowledgement are essential... It is the victims themselves who must speak."[7] The Promotion of National Unity and Reconciliation Act 34 of 1995 then established the TRC.

The main task of the TRC was to investigate human rights **violations** from 1960 to 1994. These dates were chosen so that victims of the violence between the ANC and the IFP could tell their stories, in addition to people who had been harmed by the apartheid government. The TRC would offer amnesty to perpetrators if they met certain conditions. In addition, it would construct a historical record by providing an account of its findings that would be available to all. It would make recommendations to prevent future human rights abuses. The TRC would have three committees: a Human Rights Violations Committee, an Amnesty Committee, and a **Reparations** and **Rehabilitation** Committee.

The Promotion of National Unity and Reconciliation Act defined "gross human rights violations" as torture, killings, disappearances, and abductions (seizing people illegally), in addition to severe bad treatment suffered at the hands of the

The three committees of the TRC

Chair: Archbishop Desmond Tutu
Deputy Chair: Alex Boraine

Human Rights Violations Committee

Task: to investigate the gross violations of human rights under apartheid in South Africa and outside from 1960 to 1994

Amnesty Committee

Task: to receive applications for amnesty, organize hearings, and decide whether applicants should be given amnesty

Reparations and Rehabilitation Committee

Task: to assess the amount and type of reparation that victims should receive

In 1995, Ntsiki Biko, the wife of Steve Biko (see pages 18–19), lays a wreath on the floor where Biko is believed to have died in Pretoria Central Prison. The TRC would unveil the truth behind many similar deaths in custody.

apartheid state. It would also include violations committed by the liberation movement. These crimes represented just a small proportion of the human rights abuses inflicted on the population under apartheid.

Selecting the commissioners

Who would be the commissioners to run the process? Mandela opted not to make the decision himself, but rather to adopt a democratic selection process. Organizations such as political parties, churches, and individuals submitted nominations (suggestions) to a committee, which drew up a short list of names. Mandela and his cabinet selected 17 commissioners from the short list. He appointed Archbishop Tutu, who was strongly committed to reconciliation (see pages 28 and 29), as the chair (head) of the commission.

What do you think?

Was it right for the TRC to focus on gross human rights violations?

Those who believed that it was right to focus on gross human rights violations argued that it would have taken many years to investigate all the human rights abuses. This would have been impractical and expensive. However, others argued that the narrow focus of the TRC meant that a huge number of people who had suffered terribly under apartheid – for example, being forced from their homes or harassed by the police – did not have the chance to air their grievances.

The TRC gets to work

At the Johannesburg hearing, Hawa Timoi described the pain she experienced after security forces killed her son Ahmed, saying: "I told the police that if my body had a zip they could open the zip to see how I was aching inside."[1]

Timoi was just one of more than 22,000 victims who made statements to the Human Rights Violations Committee.[2] The committee employed people to record the statements and to listen to people's stories in their own language, with empathy and respect. The statement-takers recorded the details in English. An interview often took several hours and was an intense and painful experience for both parties. The process allowed people to express feelings, in addition to providing facts. They were able to share their burden.

The Human Rights Violations Committee drew on the statements from victims to find out how and why the abuses took place, who was responsible, and the harm the victims suffered.

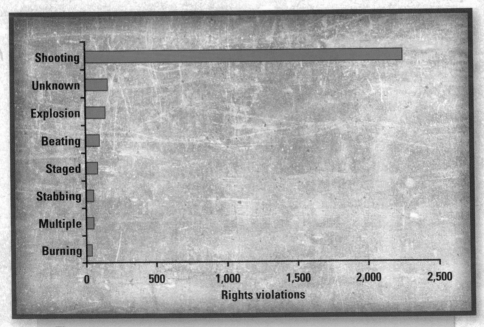

The police commonly beat their victims. They also used physical and psychological torture. This graph indicates the type of killings carried out by the South African police forces from 1960 to 1994.

Public hearings

From the statements, representative cases were selected to present at public hearings, to ensure that each gender, race, age, and location, and all sides of the conflict were represented. At the hearings, victims **testified** in front of commissioners, friends, family, the media, and other interested parties. The majority were victims of the apartheid regime, but others had suffered at the hands of the liberation movement, including the ANC, PAC, and IFP.

Victims spoke of the ongoing trauma they had endured. For example, Madala Ndlazi described how his 16-year-old son was shot by the police on 16 June 1986, saying:

> "I found my child brought to the home. I found him in the dining room. He was lying dead there in the dining room. When I looked at him, it was very painful for me to see how injured he was. My wife and I knew he would die … but the way in which my son was injured, makes me very painful. I cannot forget this. It is almost ten years now."[3]

Beth Savage's story

White people spoke at the hearings, too. Beth Savage recounted that in 1992, she was enjoying a Christmas party at the King William's Town Golf Club, near East London, when members of the armed wing of the PAC burst in and hurled hand grenades (small bombs) into the room. Savage was hit by an exploding grenade and required months of medical treatment to recover from wounds caused by shrapnel (the small pieces of metal thrown out by the grenade).

After finishing her account, Savage said: "I would like to meet the man that threw the grenade in an attitude of forgiveness and hope that he could forgive me, too." By saying this, she acknowledged that she had benefited from apartheid and bore some responsibility for it. Only a minority of white South Africans expressed such sentiments.[4]

The mother of Anton Lubowski, shown in 1996 holding up a picture of her son, a Namibian anti-apartheid campaigner who was shot dead in 1989 by an undercover South African government unit.

The Amnesty Committee

If the Human Rights Violations hearings were stressful and painful for all involved, the 2,500 amnesty hearings were even more difficult. Victims often attended and met their former tormenters face-to-face. They saw the killers of their loved ones in the flesh. Charity Kondile attended the hearing where Vlakplaas Commander Dirk Coetzee described how he murdered her son Sizwe (see below).

For perpetrators like Coetzee to receive amnesty, there were various conditions, including the following:

• The action had to have taken place between 1960 and 1994.

• It had to be politically motivated.

• The applicant had to disclose (reveal) all the facts.

If these conditions were met, then amnesty could be granted. The conditions for amnesty were controversial, because perpetrators did not even have to apologize – although many did. But they did have to admit they were guilty of horrendous acts towards other human beings. Victims, friends, family, and the public would know exactly what they had done.

The crimes of Dirk Coetzee

Members of the security forces came forward to give evidence. Many were in prison and hoped to be given amnesty and released. One was Dirk Coetzee. He had worked for Vlakplaas, the unit of the South African police force that hunted down and killed opponents of the

Dirk Coetzee, the former Vlakplaas commander who was granted amnesty for the murder of Griffiths Mxenge, pictured in Durban, 1996.

apartheid government. He revealed involvement in 23 incidents, 14 of which included gross violations of human rights.

Coetzee had been convicted of the gruesome murder of Griffiths Mxenge, a human rights lawyer who had been hacked to death in 1981. He then described in detail how he and his Vlakplaas colleagues had killed a student activist from the Eastern Cape, Sizwe Kondile, in the same year. To destroy the evidence of the murder, they decided to burn the body. Coetzee explained:

> "The burning of a body on an open fire takes seven hours. Whilst that happened we were drinking and braaing [barbecuing] next to the fire. I tell this not to hurt the family, but to show you the callousness [uncaring way] with which we did things in those days."[5]

Despite the horrific nature of his crimes, Coetzee was given amnesty because it was clear he had acted on "the advice, command, or order of one or more senior members of the Security Branch".[6]

The conviction of "Prime Evil"

Most perpetrators did not receive amnesty, and some were **prosecuted**. Eugene de Kock, nicknamed "Prime Evil" in the media, was the commander of Vlakplaas and bore the responsibility for the kidnapping, torture, and murder of anti-apartheid activists in the 1980s and early 1990s. He revealed the extent of his crimes to the TRC, but as the commander, he could not receive amnesty. De Kock was put on trial and sentenced to 212 years in prison.[7] Despite high-profile cases like this one, many perpetrators were never brought to justice.

Amnesty applications
The following table shows facts about amnesty applications, up to 1988:

Total applications received	7,060
Total dealt with	4,696
Amnesty granted	125
Amnesty refused	4,571[8]

Challenges to the TRC

Some people affected by the conflict refused to accept the TRC. The top levels of the military and security forces and many senior politicians failed to come forward. They argued that the TRC did not understand the perspectives of people at the time, who had been brought up in the apartheid system and were taught to defend it. This led them to carry out human rights violations, they argued.

Military versus politicians

The military forces and the politicians blamed each other for the abuses. For instance, former Police Minister Adriaan Vlok claimed that President de Klerk had ordered the torture and killing of political opponents. De Klerk denied this. He stated that government strategies "never included the authorization of assassination, murder, torture, rape, assault, or the like".[9] Yet former Foreign Affairs Minister Pik Botha admitted that cabinet ministers suspected the police were torturing and killing opponents, but they did nothing about it.

At least de Klerk was prepared to speak to the TRC. Former President Botha vehemently resisted attempts to call him to account, calling it a "circus" at which he would not perform. Mandela went out of his way to persuade Botha to testify before the commission. He even offered to accompany

Decisive words: Orders to kill?

Police and army officers at the amnesty hearings mentioned documents that called for the "elimination", "neutralization", or "removing from society" of opponents. They had interpreted these terms to mean they should kill their enemies. Former Police Minister Adriaan Vlok admitted: "We at the top ... used certain terminology without thinking about it." He later claimed that President de Klerk had told the security forces they were allowed to torture and kill. Yet de Klerk would never admit to this.[11]

The police drag a protester during anti-apartheid demonstrations in Soweto in 1980. Police officers commonly used excessive force against black opponents of the government.

him to the hearing. This is especially notable, given that it was Botha's NP government that had locked up Mandela for 27 years. This incident illustrates the depth of Mandela's desire for reconciliation. Yet Botha still refused to appear before the TRC.[10]

Opinion poll 1996: Will the TRC promote reconciliation?

Respondents	% yes
African	70
Asian	59
Coloured	53
White	26[12]

As this opinion poll shows, white people had the most doubts that the TRC would be effective.

Afrikaners in shock

Many ordinary Afrikaners were furious with the TRC, writing letters to the media denying that the revelations were true and claiming the commission was biased (holding opinions against them). Large numbers claimed they simply did not know about the brutal treatment of the black majority. It was extraordinarily difficult for them to absorb the information and accept what had happened. This could only happen over time.

Buthelezi criticizes the TRC

Buthelezi (see pages 21 and 24) was also extremely critical of the TRC, believing it to be an ANC set-up and therefore biased. When he did appear in September 1996, he claimed that the IFP was innocent of any wrongdoing. However, during the human rights violations hearings, a multitude of victims testified to the abuses committed by his movement.

Evidence against the IFP

A man called Mr Mzelemu explained to the TRC how he had lost most of his family. On 2 April 1994, he heard IFP men knocking on his door. Terrified, he leapt out of the window and ran to the police station. But by the time he returned with the security forces, he was too late. The IFP had murdered his mother, his first wife, and seven of his daughters. His second wife survived, but their five-month-old baby had been stabbed and killed. The reason for the attack was that the IFP thought Mr. Mzelemu's son was involved with the ANC.[13]

The ANC is held responsible

In addition to individual hearings, the TRC organized special hearings with state institutions, businesses, media, religious organizations, and political parties. The ANC was among the organizations that had to account for its actions.

The ANC had to answer to accusations of various human rights abuses. For example, the ANC ran the Quatro prison camp in Luanda, Angola (another southern African country). It sent suspected enemies there to be "re-educated" to support the ANC. But at the TRC, former inmates gave evidence of gross violations of human rights there. The IFP, PAC, and UDF were also found responsible for attacking and killing opponents.

However, many activists in the liberation movement disagreed that their actions were gross violations of human rights. They declared that they had to use any means necessary to fight the injustice of apartheid. They felt it was wrong to equate their activities with those of the South African government.

The ANC was divided over the issue. Mandela argued firmly that it was right for all organizations to be investigated. He felt that the TRC process should educate everyone and show that human rights violations should never be seen as acceptable.

What do you think?

Was it unfair to judge the liberation struggle in the same way as the apartheid government?

When Dullah Omar introduced the Promotion of National Unity and Reconciliation Bill on 17 May 1995, he stated, "We would never want to see ourselves condoning [accepting] human rights violations simply because they were committed by freedom fighters." But he also said: "It is morally and legally wrong to equate the anti-apartheid struggle for liberation and democracy with the apartheid state."[14] What do you think?

Winnie Madikizela-Mandela

Born: Bizana, Transkei,
South Africa, 1936

Role: Social worker and activist;
second wife of Nelson Mandela

Winnie Mandela in 1987, at the funeral of an MK member. She served in the ANC government in the 1990s and from 1999, but resigned when she was convicted of fraud in 2003.

Winnie Madikizela married Nelson Mandela in 1958, after he divorced his first wife, Evelyn Ntoko Mase. She undertook social and educational work and was active in the anti-apartheid movement. While Nelson was imprisoned, Winnie suffered severe harassment by the security forces, including periods in prison and exile from her home region. In the late 1980s, she employed a gang, the Mandela United Football Club, as her bodyguards in Soweto. It was alleged that its young members were involved in the assault and rape of opponents. In 1989, Winnie was linked with the kidnapping of four young black men. One of them, Stompie Seipei, was found murdered. The ANC leadership urged Winnie to disband the club, but she refused.[15] In 1991, Winnie was sentenced to prison for the attack, but on appeal, the sentence was reduced to a fine.

During the TRC hearings, victims claimed that Winnie had committed assault and even murder. The situation proved painful and awkward for Nelson Mandela. He felt great loyalty towards his wife, who had supported him through prison life, yet their relationship after he was freed was uneasy. They divorced in 1996, partly because ANC advisers believed it was difficult politically for Nelson to remain married to her, but also for personal reasons. South Africans expressed a variety of opinions about Winnie. Some supported her courage, while others denounced her.

Reparations and Rehabilitation Committee

The Reparations and Rehabilitation Committee had to work out what compensation would be fair for the victims of gross human rights violations. It came up with the following provisions (conditions):

- supplying urgent interim (short-term) payment for people who were in urgent need

- giving individual reparation grants to victims

- giving symbolic reparation to help people remember their loved ones – for example, memorials such as statues or sculptures

- creating community rehabilitation programmes, such as community services to help healing

- putting in place institutional reform, to prevent the future abuse of human rights.[16]

Criticism of the committee

The Reparations and Rehabilitation Committee was heavily criticized. The amnesty hearings granted immediate release to perpetrators who were in prison, but the reparation step took a long time. This meant that victims saw their tormenters go free, but they then had to wait a long time for reparations.

For example, Mr Mzelemu, who saw most of his family murdered (see page 37), made particular requests to the commission. Unable to forget the brutal killings, he asked for counselling and for assistance to find one of his daughters, who remained missing. He also asked for financial assistance because he and his wife were unemployed. Victims like Mr Mzelemu needed practical help to try to live normal lives again.

But the committee was slow to come up with recommendations and lacked its own budget for reparations. It was up to the government to provide the money, but even the so-called interim payment was not paid until late 1998. Some commissioners donated money out of their own pockets to help victims pay for urgent necessities, such as applying for a death certificate.[17]

There was a seven-and-a-half-year delay before people received their final compensation. In 2003, more than 19,000 victims

In 2010, Khulumani (see the box below) was involved in a legal case against vehicle manufacturer Daimler, accused of selling vehicles to the apartheid government. Mamosadi Catherine Mlangeni (whose son was killed) says she was repeatedly arrested and taken to the police station in a Daimler vehicle.

received a one-time payment of 30,000 Rand (about £2,100 in today's money). In South Africa at the time, the average annual salary was just under £2,000.[18] A standard amount was offered, which did not take into account the individual needs of victims.

Some people felt this was a missed opportunity for individual reconciliation and relieving poverty. It was hard for people to forgive the perpetrators while waiting years to receive any compensation, with their lives no better than they had been under apartheid. Research indicated that the compensation received did little to help pay for the costs related to injuries or to improve the possibilities for people to lead better lives.[19]

Khulumani Support Group

Khulumani means "speaking out" in the Zulu language. The Khulumani Support Group is a social movement that was set up in 1995 to campaign for the human rights of survivors of gross human rights violations during the apartheid era. It continued to operate after the TRC, because it believed there was still work to be done. Many people had not come forward to speak to the TRC. Either they did not find out about it in time or they did not manage to make statements. Through Khulumani, these people were able to make statements after the TRC process was completed. Today, the group helps survivors of violations build their work skills, which is important because many of these people are unemployed. It also continues to lobby for the prosecution of perpetrators who did not apply for amnesty.[20]

Achievements

In October 1998, just before the publication of the TRC's report, the ANC suddenly announced the intention to stop the report from being published. Leading members of the party, such as Deputy President Thabo Mbeki, declared that the ANC had been treated unfairly. They felt that the liberation movement was being criminalized for justifiable actions against apartheid. Would the report's findings never see the light of day?

Mandela stepped in. He strongly disagreed with Mbeki and accepted the report's findings, saying: "The ANC was fighting a just war, but in the course of fighting the just war, it committed gross violations of human rights. Nobody can deny that, because some people died in our camps and that's what the TRC said."[1]

Yet Mbeki opted to take the commission to South Africa's High Court to try to prevent the publication of the report's sections about the ANC. On the morning of 29 October, the date set for the publication of the report, the commissioners gathered in Pretoria. Surrounded by restless journalists, they awaited the

President Nelson Mandela receives the five volumes of the TRC final report from Archbishop Desmond Tutu. The report was presented to parliament on 25 February 1999.

court's decision. If the court decided against the TRC, it would not be possible to make the report public to journalists and the world via the internet. Mid-morning, just two hours before the ceremony was due to begin, word came through that the High Court had ruled in favour of the commission. The report – including findings about the ANC – would be available to all.

A mixed reception

The ceremony went ahead as planned. Desmond Tutu formally handed over the 3,500-page report to Mandela. Mandela accepted it graciously, with a speech that stressed a break with the past and that promoted unity, emphasizing that the report was not a slur on any particular race.

The report was presented to parliament on 25 February 1999. Mandela again thanked the commission and made it clear that the debate about reconciliation should continue for a long time. But Mbeki restated his criticism of the commission, claiming, "One of the central matters at issue ... remains the erroneous [mistaken] determination of various actions of our liberation movements as gross violations of human rights."[2] With reactions to the report so mixed even within the government, how did others in South Africa – and worldwide – feel about it?

The report

The following were the main findings of the TRC:

- Between 1960 and 1994, the government and its security forces, including former President Botha himself, were responsible for many gross human rights violations, including torture and killings.

- The leaders of the Volksfront and the AWB (see page 25) were responsible for gross human rights violations, as was the ANC in its camps.

- The IFP, including its leader, Buthelezi, was accountable for human rights abuses committed by the KwaZulu government.

- Winnie Mandela was personally responsible for committing gross human rights violations and was responsible for the actions of the Mandela United Football Club (see page 39).[3]

- The ANC was responsible for the deaths of civilians (everyday people) in operations carried out by MK from 1961 to 1990.[4]

Negative responses to the TRC

Some people argued that large numbers of victims were left out of the truth and reconciliation process, due to the narrow focus of the commission on gross human rights violations. Millions of people suffered under apartheid, but they were not able to testify about the injustice of daily life as a black South African.

And what about the ordinary white people who benefited from apartheid? Professor Mahmood Mamdani, from the University of Cape Town, noted that in South Africa, there were relatively few perpetrators of gross human rights abuses, but there were many beneficiaries (people who benefited). He wondered whether reconciliation should take place between victims and beneficiaries.[5]

Too generous to perpetrators?

Some people claimed that the commission was altogether too generous towards perpetrators. They criticized Mandela's principle of forgiveness, which was enshrined in the TRC. Although the truth came out, justice was not done, because people who were granted amnesty could not be prosecuted for their crimes. This meant that people who had committed **atrocities** got away with their actions. Also, a large proportion of applicants did not receive amnesty, but a few were then tried in court. This appeared to make a mockery of the amnesty system.

The TRC found that members of the far-right AWB were responsible for violence. Here, AWB members are seen attacking the South African police at a rally in Ventersdorp, west of Johannesburg, in 1991.

Another criticism was that although many perpetrators spoke out, the process failed to target the decision makers – the politicians and the leaders of the security forces who were responsible for the apartheid system. Therefore it was the "trigger pullers" – the people on the ground who actually carried out the policies – who took the blame for abuses, rather than the people who formed the policies.

The rich-poor divide

Some people felt that the huge gap between rich and poor in South Africa meant that the TRC alone was not enough to bring about reconciliation. As deputy chairman of the commission Alex Boraine noted, "The **legacy** of apartheid includes a badly skewed economy... The healing of a nation will thus require disciplined commitment to economic growth so that the alleviation [lessening] of poverty can begin in earnest."[6] In his view, reconciliation meant little to people whose situation was just as bad as it had always been.

What do you think?

Was reconciliation possible?

Father Mxolisi Mpambani told this story during a discussion about reconciliation at the University of Cape Town. Here, the character of Tom represents white South Africans, while Bernard stands for the black majority:

"Once, there were two boys, Tom and Bernard. Tom lived right opposite Bernard. One day Tom stole Bernard's bicycle and every day Bernard saw Tom cycling to school on it. After a year, Tom went up to Bernard, stretched out his hand and said, 'Let us reconcile and put the past behind us.'

Bernard looked at Tom's hand and said, 'And what about the bicycle?'

'No,' said Tom, 'I'm not talking about the bicycle – I'm talking about reconciliation.'"[7]

Does this show that reconciliation was impossible to achieve because injustice remained? Or is this view too negative?

Positive responses to the TRC

Most people agreed that the hearings were the main strength of the TRC. Through the human rights violations hearings, victims had their say, and all South Africans became aware of past atrocities. No one could now claim they did not know what happened.

The amnesty hearings were also praised for their openness. Conditional amnesty – meaning that perpetrators must meet certain conditions to get amnesty – was considered a useful compromise, because it encouraged the perpetrators to confess their deeds honestly. Many black people finally discovered what had happened to their loved ones, and the remains of bodies were returned to families to bury with dignity.

Remarkably, no revenge attacks against perpetrators occurred after the amnesty hearings.[8] The victims clearly felt that revealing their crimes in public was punishment enough for the perpetrators. Criminal court proceedings would not have revealed the details of past abuses in the same way.

The truth at last

Joe Mamasela, who worked for Dirk Coetzee at Vlakplaas (see pages 34–35), provided evidence at the amnesty hearings. He described how he and two other Vlakplaas men had been in trouble. They had borrowed money from Coetzee to buy diamonds in Lesotho. When they returned, Coetzee said they had been cheated and should return the diamonds. The men knew the diamond dealer would refuse to return the money, but they could not return to Coetzee with nothing. At the Lesotho border, they decided to kill the next man who came along, steal his car, and give it to Coetzee instead of the money – and that is what they did. After the story was broadcast on the radio, someone called the station from Lesotho to say, "Thank you Radio Lesesi, thank you Mamasela – we've been wondering for years what happened to our father."[10]

Praised abroad

Internationally, the truth and reconciliation process was regarded as successful. People were astounded by the dramatic accounts of both victims and perpetrators, who spoke out openly and honestly. Genuine understanding between victims and perpetrators took place, setting the process of reconciliation in motion. Following the South African example, other countries have adopted similar reconciliation processes.

Mandela offers forgiveness

Mandela's personal contribution to the TRC was hugely important. He displayed an extraordinary lack of bitterness and a readiness to forgive and to focus on coming to terms with the past. In his personal life, he offered the hand of friendship to the people who had imprisoned him and tortured and oppressed his people. In 1994, when Niel Barnard retired as head of intelligence, Mandela gave a dinner party for him. The guests included General Willie Willemse, the former commander of Robben Island, who was greatly moved by the invitation and said the dinner was a "wonderful experience".[9]

President Mandela shakes hands with Bertie Verwoerd, the widow of late apartheid prime minister Hendrik Verwoerd, in 1995. Such visits won him support in the white community.

Forgiveness helps

In 2009, Olga Macingwane met Stefaans Coetzee, the bomber who had injured her when he left a pipe bomb in a Shoprite store in Worchester, Western Cape, 13 years earlier. The attack left four people dead and at least 65 injured. Coetzee and two others were found guilty of the attack and sent to prison. Macingwane had not been able to forgive Coetzee until she met him in Pretoria Central Prison. She listened to his side of the story and realized that he — only 18 years old when he carried out the attack — had been "used by apartheid". She found that she felt sorry for Coetzee and was able to forgive him. Forgiving has helped her to heal, too. She says, "It's like a load has been lifted off my shoulders."[11]

What might have been different?

What might have happened if South Africa had selected a path other than the TRC?

War crimes trials

The country could have had war crimes trials, as had occurred after the conflict in Bosnia (in southeastern Europe) between Serbs, Croats, and Muslims. In 1993, an International Criminal Tribunal was set up to judge people who were alleged to have carried out massacres in Bosnia.

If South Africa had adopted this approach, it is likely that many perpetrators would have fled the country to escape justice. The security forces, police, and politicians probably would not have cooperated with the process, making it ineffective. More seriously, if the security forces had been challenged in this way, they might not have remained loyal to the government. The violence of the early 1990s could have propelled South Africa into civil war. However, some critics believe that war crimes trials should nevertheless have taken place.

General amnesty

Another option would have been to grant general amnesty, as in the Democratic Republic of Congo. In 2009, the president there

War crimes trials would have been better

Professor Richard Goldstone, a justice of the Constitutional Court of South Africa, contended in 2007 that there should have been war crimes trials there, saying:

"There can be no question that apartheid was a most serious crime against humanity… I don't believe that South Africa would have got away with the amnesty provisions of the TRC today. I think that the [new] International Criminal Court [set up to prosecute people for crimes against humanity] and the attitude of most of the democratic world towards crimes of that magnitude [size] would make it virtually impossible to allow for amnesties for the army and police leaders who behaved as they did. I would prefer to see trials rather than amnesties in that sort of situation. South Africa just got away with it in 1995 and I think there were a lot of reasons for that. It was the attitude of Nelson Mandela, his popularity, and it was also very importantly the wish of the majority of the victims in South Africa to go that route; but the world has changed since then."[13]

brought in an amnesty law forgiving all fighters for war-related violence during the civil conflict from 2003 to 2009. However, human rights organizations such as Amnesty International criticized the law, because it allowed the crimes of rebel groups, police, and armed forces to go unpunished.[12] If a similar law had been introduced in South Africa, perpetrators would have avoided admitting their crimes publicly and would have enjoyed impunity (lack of punishment) through the law. Victims would have had no chance to tell their story.

No action

Alternatively, the government could have ignored the issue completely in the interest of "moving on". This would have denied both victims and perpetrators their say and the possibility of meeting and coming to understand each other.

Reconciliation is right

Cynthia Ngewu is the mother of Christopher Piet, an anti-apartheid activist in MK who was one of seven young men killed by the government security forces in 1986. She said:

"This thing called reconciliation… if I am understanding it correctly… if it means this perpetrator, this man who has killed Christopher Piet, if it means he becomes human again, this man, so that I, so that all of us, get our humanity back…then I agree, then I support it all."[14]

Members of the army in the Democratic Republic of Congo, during the civil conflict of 2003–2009. The amnesty law did not stop the fighting, which continued in the east of the country.

Mandela's legacy

Mandela took over a divided country and worked to turn it into a "rainbow" nation that included people of different colours. All adults could vote for the government, which had representatives from all races. People from all backgrounds could apply for government jobs. South Africa was welcomed back into the family of nations, and other nations ended their economic boycotts and sanctions. A highlight of this time of healing was Mandela's support for the South African rugby union team, the Springboks, in the rugby union World Cup.

Social and economic problems

Grand gestures such as Mandela's support of the Springboks were significant, but daily life for ordinary people in South Africa changed little. There was still a huge gap in living standards between black and white people. Mandela introduced an ambitious economic plan, the Reconstruction and Development Programme. It aimed to build schools and homes, provide electricity and clean water supplies, and create new jobs for the poverty-stricken black population.

However, the economic reforms did not have a dramatic effect. Most white businesses did not greatly change the racial balance of their workers.[1] In general, whites remained wealthier and had

The 1995 Rugby World Cup

Beginning in the 1970s, many countries boycotted South African sports, refusing to play matches against South African teams. But after 1994, the country's athletes were excited to be able to play international matches again.

In South Africa, rugby union was associated with Afrikaners and white arrogance, and the South African team, the Springboks, had just one non-white team member (who was "coloured").

The World Cup final took place on 24 June 1995, between South Africa and New Zealand. The World Cup was South Africa's first international sports event since the fall of apartheid. The Springboks went on to win. Mandela was one of the spectators. At the end, he walked on to the pitch and presented rugby captain François Pienaar with the trophy. The mostly Afrikaner audience went wild with delight, and Mandela's actions endeared him to millions of rugby fans.[3] The story was dramatized in the film *Invictus* in 2009.

better jobs, while black people experienced poorer living conditions, schooling, and job prospects than whites. At the start of the 21st century, around 50 per cent of the population existed in poverty, and about 24 per cent was unemployed.[2] Socially, the majority mostly mixed with people of the same race for leisure and recreation. Social problems afflicted South Africa, too, including a dramatic rise in the number of people infected with the HIV virus that causes **AIDS**, in addition to high crime levels.

President Nelson Mandela and deputy President Thabo Mbeki at an ANC election rally in Soweto, 30 May 1999. The ANC remained in power for the following decade.

But when Mandela handed over the presidency in 1999, to Mbeki, he passed on a working democracy. This democracy had a distinctly African character, reflecting the majority (black) population. Serious difficulties clearly remained, but they might have been worse if the truth and reconciliation process had not taken place. Mandela's support for the TRC was therefore one of his important legacies.

President Mandela, wearing a Springboks shirt, presents the Rugby World Cup trophy to South Africa captain François Pienaar.

Mandela and conflict resolution

After Mbeki became president, Mandela continued to work for conflict resolution. He founded the Nelson Mandela Foundation in 1999. In 2004, he founded the Centre of Memory, which documents Mandela's life and promotes a dialogue around important social issues in order to promote justice. Mandela also became involved in international reconciliation work. He was a founding member of the Elders in 2007, a group of world leaders promoting conflict resolution. He mediated in (helped resolve) other conflicts – for example, in Northern Ireland.[4]

Breaking the silence over AIDS

Mandela continued to get involved within South Africa, too, notably with the AIDS crisis, which had reached epidemic (extremely widespread) proportions during his presidency. In 2005, Mandela's son Makgatho died of AIDS, and Mandela made a public statement to this effect. This was a break with the normal policy. Up until then, people would choose to name a related disease – such as tuberculosis – as the cause of death, rather than admitting a loved one had died of AIDS.[5] Mandela wanted to bring the problem of AIDS out in the open, so that people with HIV could access treatment to control the condition.

South African President F.W. de Klerk and Nelson Mandela hold up medals and certificates after they were jointly awarded the Nobel Peace Prize in December 1993.

Mandela's talent for negotiation

In addition to considering Mandela's later work in promoting social change and reconciliation, it is important to look back at his legacy as ANC leader. Despite his long years in prison, Mandela played a key role in the leadership of the liberation movement. In particular, he can be credited with steering South Africa towards a peaceful democratic solution after 1990. Leading ANC and SACP member Joe Slovo believed it was Mandela more than anyone who persuaded the ANC to abandon the armed struggle and accept negotiations with the regime, saying: "When it came to facing the post-1990 period, the role of Mandela is absolutely unique."[6] Arguably, this was his most important legacy.

Mandela and forgiveness

Mandela's third wife, Graça Machel (whom he married in 1998), saw South African forgiveness as widespread – it was part of African culture to forgive. But she believed that Mandela's leadership had been crucial to promoting this view, saying:

> "If he had come out of prison and sent a different message, I can tell you this country could be in flames… He knew exactly the way he wanted to come out, but also the way he addressed the people … sending the message of what he thought was the best way to save lives in this country, to bring reconciliation."[8]

In more general terms, however, perhaps Mandela's greatest legacy lies in his ability to work with all kinds of people. In prison, he acquired the ability to sit down and talk patiently with people from every walk of life and explain the justness of his cause.[7] He learnt to never become angry and to always understand another person's point of view. It was his extraordinary capacity for empathy (understanding the feelings of others) that led him to support the TRC. Mandela's ability to see the good in people, to work with them no matter their differences, and to find a compromise helped to ensure the transition from apartheid to democracy in South Africa.

What do you think?

What was Mandela's most important legacy?

How significant was the TRC as part of Mandela's legacy?
Were his previous achievements more important?

Timeline

1910
The Union of South Africa is formed as an independent country

1912
Representatives of black organizations form the South African Native National Congress, which from 1923 is known as the African National Congress (ANC)

1913
Under the Natives' Land Act, 7 per cent of South Africa's land is set aside for the majority black population

1914
The National Party (NP) is formed to fight for Afrikaner rights

1918
Nelson Mandela is born

1961
June
The ANC decides to set up Umkhonto we Sizwe (MK), to carry out sabotage

1960
21 March
The police kill 69 protesters at a demonstration in Sharpeville

1958
March
Mandela divorces Evelyn Ntoko Mase
June
Mandela marries Winnie Madikizela
September
Hendrik Verwoerd becomes prime minister and promotes the Bantustan policy

1956
December
The government arrests 156 leaders of the anti-apartheid movement, including Mandela

1962
August
Mandela is arrested

1964
12 June
Mandela and several other ANC leaders are sentenced to life imprisonment. They are sent to Robben Island.

1975
Mangosutho Buthelezi sets up the Inkatha movement

1976
16 June
During the Soweto Uprising, the police fire on protesters, killing two children

1977
18 August
The police arrest Steve Biko; he dies in police custody five days later

1978
September
P.W. Botha becomes prime minister

1992
Mandela sets up a consultation group to discuss a truth commission
March
In a referendum of the white population, 69 per cent of voters support the negotiations toward dismantling apartheid
17 June
IFP activists raid the township of Boipatong, near Vereeniging, killing 46 people
26 September
The government and the ANC sign a Record of Understanding

1991
July
Mandela becomes president of the ANC
20 December
The first meeting of the Convention for a Democratic South Africa (CODESA) takes place

1993
The ANC decides to set up a truth commission
May
The Volksfront forms. It is an alliance of right-wing groups that demand a separate Afrikaner nation.

1994
27 April
The ANC wins the first multiracial elections
10 May
Mandela becomes the president of South Africa
27 May
Minister of Justice Dullah Omar announces to parliament the decision to set up the Truth and Reconciliation Commission (TRC)

1921
The South African Communist Party (SACP) is formed

1944
Mandela joins the ANC and becomes leader of the Youth League

He marries Evelyn Ntoko Mase

1948
The NP wins the South African elections and introduces the system of apartheid

1949
The Prohibition of Mixed Marriages Act makes it illegal for white people to marry members of other racial groups

1950
The Population Registration Act categorizes people into four racial groups: white, coloured (mixed race), Asiatic (Indian), and native (African)

The Group Areas Act creates separate living areas for the different races

1955
June
The Congress of the People is held in Kliptown, near Johannesburg, and adopts the Freedom Charter

1952
December
Mandela and Oliver Tambo set up a law practice in Johannesburg

1952
April
The ANC and the South African Indian Congress lead a Defiance Campaign against the apartheid laws

1951
The Bantu Authorities Act aims to force black people to live in a Bantustan, or "homeland", meaning the area that they originally came from

1982
April
Mandela is moved to Pollsmoor Prison, along with three other senior ANC leaders

1983
20 August
A range of anti-apartheid groups form an alliance called the United Democratic Front (UDF)

1984
September
Botha introduces a new constitution that offers some political rights to coloured people and Indians

1985
20 July
Botha declares a State of Emergency, banning many organizations
1 December
The Congress of South African Trade Unions (COSATU) is formed to coordinate the activities of the black trade unions

1990
2 February
De Klerk overturns the ban on the ANC, Pan Africanist Congress (PAC), SACP, and other anti-apartheid organizations
11 February
De Klerk releases Mandela from prison
July
Buthelezi turns the Inkatha movement into a political party, called the Inkatha Freedom Party (IFP)

1989
14 September
F.W. de Klerk is elected president of South Africa

1988
Mandela begins private negotiations with members of Botha's government

1995
17 May
The Promotion of National Unity and Reconciliation Act 34 establishes the TRC

1996
15 April
The TRC public hearings begin
Mandela divorces his wife, Winnie

1997
September
Winnie Mandela appears before the TRC
Botha refuses to testify to the TRC

1998
The commission hearings end. The TRC report is published.
Mandela marries his third wife, Graça Machel, the widow of the former Mozambican president Samora Machel

2003
Victims finally receive compensation from the Reparations and Rehabilitation Committee

Notes on sources

The first witness speaks out (pages 4–5)

1. Nohle Mohape, "Truth and Reconciliation Commission Report", 15 April 1996, http://www.justice.gov.za/trc/hrvtrans/hrvel1/mohape.htm.
2. Ibid.
3. Ibid.

Mandela: an activist against apartheid (pages 6–11)

1. Cath Senker, South Africa's Anti-Apartheid Movement (Chicago: World Book, 2011), 6.
2. Patience Coster, The Struggle Against Apartheid (London: Arcturus, 2010), 19.
3. Anthony Sampson, Mandela: The Authorised Biography (London: HarperCollins, 2011), 67.
4. The Freedom Charter, June 26, 1955.
5. South African History Online, "Lilian Masediba Ngoyi", http://www.sahistory.org.za/people/lilian-masediba-ngoyi.
6. Gillian Anstey, "Isolated for Two Decades", Sunday Times Heritage Project, http://heritage.thetimes.co.za/memorials/gp/LilianNgoyi/article.aspx?id=560897.

Violent struggle (pages 12–15)

1. Heather Deagan, The Politics of the New South Africa (Harlow: Pearson Education, 2001), 31.
2. Senker, South Africa's Anti-Apartheid Movement, 27.
3. Mandela, Long Walk to Freedom, 321–22.
4. Nelson Mandela, "Statement from the Dock", 20 April 1964, www.guardian.co.uk/world/2007/apr/23/nelsonmandela1.

The tide turns (pages 16–21)

1. Sampson, Mandela: The Authorised Biography, 229.
2. Ibid., 337
3. Hilda Bernstein, "Two South Africans from the Island", In These Times, 18 January 1978, cited in Sampson, Mandela: The Authorised Biography, 229.
4. Awesome Stories, "Soweto Eyewitness: Antoinette Sithole", http://www.awesomestories.com/assets/eyewitness-antoinette-sithole.
5. Steve Biko, I Write What I Like (Oxford: Heinemann Educational Publishers, 1987), 29.
6. Sampson, Mandela: The Authorised Biography, 243 and 275.
7. Ibid., 437.

Negotiating democracy (pages 22–25)

1. Senker, South Africa's Anti-Apartheid Movement, 52.
2. Sampson, Mandela: The Authorised Biography, 436–37.
3. Ibid., 461.
4. Padraig O'Malley, "SA 1994 Post-Election Cabinet Overview", Nelson Mandela Centre of Memory and Dialogue, http://www.nelsonmandela.org/omalley/index.php/site/q/03lv02167/04lv02175/05lv02176.htm.

Setting up the Truth and Reconciliation Commission (pages 26–31)

1. Encyclopaedia Britannica, "Nürnberg Trials", http://library.eb.co.uk/eb/article-9056532?query=Nuremberg%20trials&ct=.

2. Alex Boraine, *A Country Unmasked* (Oxford: Oxford University Press, 2000), 12.

3. Antije Krog, *Country of My Skull* (London: Jonathan Cape, 1998), 12.

4. Sampson, *Mandela: The Authorised Biography*, 529.

5. Senker, *South Africa's Anti-Apartheid Movement*, 56.

6. Stacey Vee, "Desmond Tutu–Archbishop, Human Rights Activist and South African Icon", About South Africa, 23 November 2010, http://about-south-africa.com/home/culture/65-desmond-tutu-archbishop-human-rights-activist-and-south-african-icon.

7. Boraine, *A Country Unmasked*, 41.

The TRC gets to work (pages 32–41)

1. Boraine, *A Country Unmasked*, 41.

2. *Encyclopaedia Britannica*, "Truth and Reconciliation Commission, South Africa", http://library.eb.co.uk/eb/article-288202.

3. Deagan, *The Politics of the New South Africa*, 142.

4. Boraine, *A Country Unmasked*, 104.

5. Krog, *Country of My Skull*, 60.

6. South African Government Information, "Statement from the TRC on Amnesty Granted to Dirk Coetzee", 4 August 1997, http://www.info.gov.za/speeches/1997/08050w13297.htm.

7. BBC News, "The Voice of 'Prime Evil'", 28 October 1998, http://news.bbc.co.uk/1/hi/special_report/1998/10/98/truth_and_reconciliation/143668.stm.

8. Deagan, *The Politics of the New South Africa*, 156.

9. Sampson, *Mandela: The Authorised Biography*, 531.

10. Boraine, *A Country Unmasked*, 202.

11. Sampson, *Mandela: The Authorised Biography*, 530–31.

12. Deagan, *The Politics of the New South Africa*, 141.

13. Report of the Reparations and Rehabilitation Committee, "The Argument for Reparations: What the Witnesses Say", http://www.info.gov.za/otherdocs/2003/trc/2_4.pdf.

14. Boraine, *A Country Unmasked*, 69.

15. Sampson, *Mandela: The Authorised Biography*, 374–78.

16. Boraine, *A Country Unmasked*, 336.

17. *Ibid.*, 335.

18. Ginger Thompson, "South Africa to Pay $3,900 to Each Family of Apartheid Victims", New York Times, 16 April 2003, http://www.nytimes.com/2003/04/16/world/south-africa-to-pay-3900-to-each-family-of-apartheid-victims.html.

19. Traces of Truth, "Reparations", University of Witwatersrand, http://truth.wwl.wits.ac.za/cat_descr.php?cat=4.

20. Khulumani Support Group, "Who We Are", http://www.khulumani.net/khulumani/about-us/item/1-background.html.

Achievements (pages 42–49)

1. *The Sunday Times* (South Africa), 1 November 1998, cited in Deagan, *The Politics of the New South Africa*, 158.

2. Boraine, *A Country Unmasked*, 320–21.

3. Deagan, *The Politics of the New South Africa*, 159.

4. Report of the Reparations and Rehabilitation Committee, "Findings and Recommendations: Holding the ANC Accountable", http://www.info.gov.za/otherdocs/2003/trc/5_3.pdf.

5. Krog, *Country of My Skull*, 112.

6. Boraine, *A Country Unmasked*, 44.

7. Krog, *Country of My Skull*, 109.

8. *Ibid.*, 111.

9. Sampson, *Mandela: The Authorised Biography*, 522–23.

10. Krog, *Country of My Skull*, 64.

11.   Khulumani Support Group, "Forgiveness Helps, Says Bomb Victim", 20 October 2011, http://www.khulumani. net/reconciliation/item/566-forgiveness-helps-says-bomb-victim.html.

12.   International Centre for Transitional Justice, "Amnesty Must Not Equal Impunity: Focus: 2009 DRC Amnesty Law", 2009, http://ictj.org/sites/default/files/ICTJ-DRC-Amnesty-Facts-2009-English.pdf.

13.   Richard Goldstone, "Do War Crimes Trials Do More Harm Than Good?" Centre for the Study of Human Rights, London School of Economics, 2007, http://www2.lse.ac.uk/humanRights/articlesAndTranscripts/WarCrimeTrials.pdf.

14.   Krog, *Country of My Skull*, 109.

Mandela's legacy (pages 50–53)

1.   Sampson, *Mandela: The Authorised Biography*, 525.

2.   Central Intelligence Agency, "The World Fact Book: South Africa", https://www.cia.gov/library/publications/the-world-factbook/geos/sf.html.

3.   Sampson, Mandela: *The Authorised Biography*, 524.

4.   *Ibid.*, 592.

5.   *Ibid.*, 590–91.

6.   *Ibid.*, 475.

7.   *Ibid.*, 608.

8.   *Ibid.*, 533.

Glossary

African National Congress (ANC) political party set up in South Africa in 1912 to fight for black rights

Afrikaans language spoken by Afrikaners

Afrikaner white South African of European, usually Dutch, origins

AIDS stands for "Acquired Immune Deficiency Syndrome", an illness that attacks the body's ability to resist infection. Without treatment, AIDS usually causes death.

amnesty statement that allows people who have committed political crimes to go free. It may be conditional, which means the applicants have to meet certain conditions, or it can be general, which allows everyone who committed the crimes to go free.

apartheid political system in South Africa that divided people into four "races": white, coloured, Indian, and black. Each race had to live, work, and socialize separately. Only white people had full political rights.

atrocity cruel and violent act

banning order order banning someone from particular activities, such as meeting other people or making speeches

Bantustan under apartheid, there were Bantustans, or "homelands", for black people, who were supposed to live in the Bantustan they came from. Black people were only allowed to own land in a Bantustan (see also "homelands").

Black Consciousness movement South African movement in the 1970s that encouraged black people to take pride in themselves and their culture. It included all non-white people who suffered from racism under apartheid.

boycott organized effort to weaken a country by refusing to trade with it or play sports matches with its teams

cabinet group of members of a government who are responsible for advising and deciding on government policy

charter statement describing the rights that a particular group of people should have

civil war war between groups of people in the same country

coloured South African term under apartheid used to define people of mixed heritage (those who had one black and one white parent)

communist person who supports communism, the system of government in which the government controls the production of goods and the running of services

compensation award, usually of money, given to someone because he or she has been hurt

constitution set of laws governing a country or organization

democracy system of government in which eligible citizens of a country can vote to elect their representatives

economic sanction official order that limits trade and contacts with a particular country, in order to make it do something, such as obey international law

exile being sent or deciding to live in another country or part of the country, particularly for political reasons

homeland country where a person was born. In South Africa under apartheid, the government declared that the area of a country where a black person was born was his or her homeland. Not every black person had a homeland, however. There were black people who were born in towns and had never been in a homeland.

Inkatha movement that Mangosutho Buthelezi set up in KwaZulu in 1975 to fight for Zulu rights

Inkatha Freedom Party (IFP) Buthelezi's political party, established in 1990 to fight for an independent KwaZulu homeland within South Africa

legacy situation that exists now because of events that took place in the past

liberation freedom of a country from rule by another country. In South Africa under apartheid, liberation meant freedom from rule by the white minority.

massacre killing of a large number of people in a cruel way

National Party (NP) political party founded in South Africa in 1914 to fight for Afrikaner rights. After it won the election in 1948, it brought in the apartheid system.

Nazi member of the National Socialist party that ruled Germany from 1933 to 1945

Pan Africanist Congress (PAC) organization of black campaigners, founded in South Africa in 1959 by Robert Sobukwe, to fight the apartheid government. Sobukwe broke away from the multiracial ANC, believing that the anti-apartheid struggle was a black African struggle and so black Africans must do it alone.

parliament group of people who are elected to make and change the laws of a country

perpetrator person who commits a crime or does something that is wrong or evil

prime minister head of government in South Africa between 1910 and 1984

prosecute officially charge somebody with a crime in court

reconciliation end to a conflict and the restoring of good relationships

regime system of government, especially one that has not been elected in a fair way

rehabilitation process of helping somebody to have a normal, useful life again after he or she has been very ill for a long time

reparation act of giving something to somebody or doing something for the person in order to show that you are sorry for suffering that you have caused

sabotage causing deliberate damage to buildings, equipment, or transport in order to protest against something

South African Communist Party (SACP) party formed in 1921 in South Africa to fight for black rights, it struggled against apartheid alongside the ANC. It followed communist principles.

testify make a statement that something happened, especially as a witness in court

township town on the edge of a South African city where non-white people lived under apartheid and continue to live today. Each group – the blacks, coloureds, and Indians – lived in their own township.

trade union organization of workers that exists to protect their interests and improve their working conditions

treason crime of doing something that could cause danger to your country

United Democratic Front (UDF) alliance formed by a range of anti-apartheid groups in South Africa in 1983 to campaign against the apartheid government

violation in a human rights context, the failure to respect people's human rights. A gross violation is an extremely serious violation – for example, seriously injuring or killing people.

war crime cruel act that is committed during a war and goes against the international rules of war

Find out more

Books

Non-fiction

Desmond Tutu: A Biography, Steven D. Gish (Greenwood, 2004)

Nelson Mandela, Bob Shone (Franklin Watts, 2009)

Nelson Mandela (Famous People), Hakim Adi (Wayland, 2008)

The End of Apartheid in South Africa (Milestones in Modern World History), Liz Sonneborn (Chelsea House, 2010)

The Release of Nelson Mandela (Dates with History), John Malam (Evans, 2008)

For older readers

A Country Unmasked, Alex Boraine (OUP, 2000)
Alex Boraine was the deputy chair of the TRC.

No Future Without Forgiveness: A Personal Overview of South Africa's Truth and Reconciliation Commission, Desmond Tutu (Doubleday, 1999) Desmond Tutu was the chair of the TRC.

Fiction

Afrika, Colleen Craig (Tundra, 2008)
This book is about a teenager of South African origin who visits South Africa at the time of the TRC hearings.

DVDs

Frontline: The Long Walk of Nelson Mandela (PBS, 2012) This film tells the story of Mandela's life and includes interviews with many people who have known him, including politicians, friends, and prisoners and guards from Robben Island.

Invictus (Warner Home Video, 2010) (rated PG-13) This film is about the 1995 Rugby World Cup. It was one of South Africa's first international sporting events after the fall of apartheid.

Nelson Mandela: Journey to Freedom (History Channel, 2006) This documentary about Mandela includes supplemental lessons for students.

Websites

news.bbc.co.uk/1/hi/special_report/1998/10/98/truth_and_reconciliation/203134.stm
This BBC web page has all you need to know about the Truth and Reconciliation Commission.

www.justice.gov.za/trc
The official web site of the TRC contains the final report and all the important documents from the commission.

www.nelsonmandela.org
Visit Nelson Mandela's website, which provides details about his life and his work to promote dialogue about social issues.

www.sahistory.org.za
South African History Online is a history project set up in 2000 to create a comprehensive encyclopaedia of South African history and culture.

www.southafrica.info
This is the official website of South Africa, and it includes information about Nelson Mandela and all aspects of South African society.

Other topics to research

You might like to find out more about South Africa after apartheid and life for people of different races there. You could find out about Nelson Mandela's continued work towards peace and reconciliation after the TRC. You may like to look into truth commissions in other countries – there is a list on the Amnesty International website.

Index